10 Minutes a Day
to Reading Success

activities and skill builders to help your second grader learn to love reading

Houghton Mifflin Company
Boston   New York   1998

Copyright © 1998 by Houghton Mifflin Company

Product Development: Editorial Options, Inc.
Project Editor: Gari Fairweather
Designer: Lynne Torrey, Karen Donica

Illustrations by Anthony Lewis
Pencil page spot art previously published in Houghton Mifflin's *Phonics, Books 1-5*, copyright
(c) 1997 by Houghton Mifflin Company. Pencil page art also by: Liz Callen, Roberta Holmes,
Ed Parker, Lou Vaccaro

For information about permission to reproduce selections from this book, write to Permissions,
Houghton Mifflin Company, 215 Park Avenue South, New York, New York, 10003.

ISBN 0-395-90154-5

Printed in the United States of America

DOC 10 9 8 7 6 5 4 3 2 1

Table of Contents

Introduction

Getting Started

Your child is off to second grade! You're probably wondering what you can do to help your child succeed in school. If you're like most of today's busy adults, you're juggling several projects at a time and looking to focus on those things that will *really* be helpful.

How can you reinforce what your child is learning in school? One way is to let your child see you reading. When you read, your child sees that reading is a worthwhile activity. Another way is to read with your child. When you share a book, your child not only has a chance to practice his or her reading skills but also to feel close to you. You can also share many different kinds of activities that promote literacy and are fun to do. That's where this book comes in.

Using *10 Minutes a Day to Reading Success*

This book contains activities you and your child can do together to reinforce concepts and skills being taught in school. Some can be completed in as little as ten minutes. Others are a bit more involved. There is no correct time limit for completing an activity, however, since each child works at his or her own pace. Look for these icons as a general guide to the amount of time an activity might take:

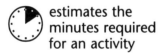 estimates the minutes required for an activity

 denotes activities requiring more than half an hour

 identifies activities centered in the kitchen

You'll find that activities with the kitchen icon make use of materials and staples found in your kitchen. Many of the other projects require materials readily found in most homes, such as crayons, markers, glue, scissors, paper, and index cards. Still other activities, like our pencil pages, invite your child to color and write in the book. Some of these pages can be completed independently, so if you need to step away for a minute, your child can continue without you.

You'll notice that the book is divided into thematic chapters designed to help your child acquire vocabulary and expand his or her knowledge base. Each chapter begins with a brief note to you that identifies the reading skills practiced in the chapter's activities. Look also for these icons, which provide information for parents, teachers, and other adults.

 Note explains a reading skill or suggests ways in which to complete an activity.

 Helping Hand provides tips for an activity, suggests alternative materials, or provides information of interest.

 More Ideas offers suggestions for other projects or ways to expand an especially enjoyable activity.

Each chapter includes a list of theme-related books you can share with your child. (You may want to gather these books early on, so you can enjoy them throughout a chapter.) At the end of each chapter is a story your child can read independently or with your help.

Feel free to photocopy or to cut up the pages. You can also use our pencil pages more than once. You might use them at the beginning of a chapter to determine how much your child already knows or use them at the end to find out how much your child has learned. Keep track of the activities your child completes by coloring in the circle at the bottom of each page.

About Learning to Read

Learning to read is a lot like learning to speak. It takes time, practice, and it's not always perfect the first time. Recall all the positive reinforcement you gave your child when he or she began to say words. Then apply this same enthusiasm, and patience, to learning to read.

In kindergarten and first grade, children learn to associate sounds and letters and to use this knowledge to decode words. For example, they learn to use the sound-letter correspondence for *p* to read words that begin with *p* (*pet*), end with *p* (*top*), and begin with the *pl* cluster (*plop*). Children also learn to use common endings, or phonograms, to read words like *bet*, *get*, *jet*, and so on. Learning sound-letter correspondences takes a lot of practice. In fact, a second-grader may spend as much time reviewing sound-letter associations introduced in the first grade as he or she will spend practicing new ones, such as the sounds for *oi* and *oy*. That's where the activities and the pencil pages in this book can help. Playing word games and practicing sound-letter associations help develop and reinforce the phonics skills your child needs to decode words.

Beginning readers also learn to use context to read new words. The broader a child's vocabulary and world knowledge, the easier it will be for him or her to understand what is being read. That's why the activities in this book are theme based — to help develop needed vocabulary and concepts. Exploring new topics with your child will help to expand your child's vocabulary and world knowledge as well.

The order in which you complete the activities in this book is up to you. You can work through one chapter, and then move on to the next. Or, you might skip around, choosing activities that appeal to your child. (Note: If your child's school uses Houghton Mifflin's reading/language arts program INVITATIONS TO LITERACY, there is a direct correspondence between the sequence of skills presented in that program and the sequence of the skills presented in this book.)

We hope you and your child will have fun. We know that finding time to do one more thing in a busy day is never easy. But by making the most of the time you do have—even ten minutes a day—you can make a big difference in your child's attitude toward reading!

Weather Watch

Weather

Whether the weather be fine,

Or whether the weather be not,

Whether the weather be cold,

Or whether the weather be hot,

We'll weather the weather

Whatever the weather,

Whether we like it or not!

Anonymous

7

A Note About Weather Watch

Most second graders are surprised to find that the first few weeks of school are easier than they anticipated when the previous year's phonics skills are reviewed. Comfortable and confident, second graders begin to look beyond the home and classroom to the larger world. In the process, they learn that reading can be used to gather information. In this chapter, children use their information-gathering skills to take a closer look at a phenomenon that affects them every day: the weather. They also review the following phonics and reading skills:

INITIAL/FINAL CONSONANTS: By second grade, children should know the sound associations for the consonant letters. These associations are briefly reviewed here and practiced throughout the book.

INITIAL CLUSTERS: Children will review and practice clusters with *l, r,* and *s.* These letter groupings may also be called *blends.*

INITIAL/FINAL DIGRAPHS: Youngsters will also practice the digraphs *sh, th,* and *ch* in initial and final positions. Unlike clusters, which blend sounds, these letter pairs form a single, new sound.

NOTING DETAILS: While reading, second graders have learned to look for important details in a story's text and pictures that help explain the story line. They are also learning to look for details in the world around them—details that help them learn and broaden their experiences.

DRAWING CONCLUSIONS: Children are learning to use information and their prior experiences to draw conclusions. If someone enters class with a dripping umbrella and a wet raincoat, they can conclude that it is raining outside. Your child can practice drawing conclusions while you read together and as situations arise during the day.

In addition to practicing reading skills, your child will practice reading strategies. One strategy is *making predictions,* which means guessing what a book might be about, based on its title and illustrations. It also means guessing what might happen next in a story. You and your child can practice this strategy when you share a book or when you try to predict the weather.

Introduce *Weather Watch* and the pig mascot for this book by sharing the poem on page 7.

Whatever the Weather

What's your favorite weather? Does sunshine make you sing? Do you like splashing in the rain? How about catching snowflakes on your tongue? Well, here's a way to have fun whatever the weather!

🕐 Weather Wheel

A weather wheel is easy to make and a great way to let the whole family know what the day's weather will be. Here's how you can make a weather wheel like the one on this page:

- Draw three lines on a paper plate so you have six equal sections.
- In each section, draw a kind of weather and label it. (Look at the weather wheel for ideas.)
- With a metal fastener, poke a hole in the center of the plate and attach two paper arrows to the weather wheel.
- Now you can move the arrows to show the weather for each day.

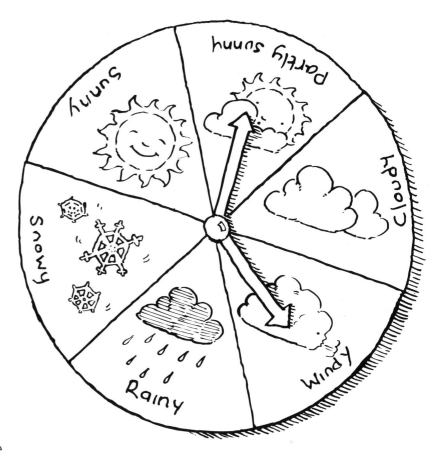

🕐 Weather Words

Listen to weather reports or look at newspaper forecasts to begin a list of weather words. Ask a family member to help you group the words by the kinds of weather they name. For different kinds of rain, you might list **shower**, **drizzle**, or **downpour**. What words might you list for different kinds of snow? How about **flurries** or **blizzard**?

Note: Observe your child as he or she writes to note any difficulties with initial or final consonants. You can practice individual sound associations by helping your child list other words that begin or end with that letter.

A good substitute for the brass fastener is a thumb tack pushed through the arrows and into an eraser.

9

Weather Reporter

What do you do when you want to know the weather? Do you look outside? Maybe you listen to the weather report on the radio or on TV. Maybe you check the forecast in the newspaper. Well, here are two ways to predict the weather.

Weather Report

Today, weather forecasters have tools that help them to predict the weather. There are simple tools like wind socks and thermometers and complex tools like space satellites. Ask a grownup to help you learn about these.

Then, with a grownup, find a newspaper weather report you can read together. Next, write your own forecast of tomorrow's weather. How can weather reports help you decide what clothes to wear?

Weather Rhyme

Long ago, people predicted the weather by noting details in nature. They often made up rhymes to remember the weather patterns they noticed. What do these rhymes predict?

> If bees stay home, rain will soon come.
> If bees fly away, it'll be a fine day.

> Ring around a winter moon
> Means snow will come soon.

Look for weather patterns where you live. Can you create a rhyme to help you remember the pattern? Try writing it down!

- Start a notebook in which your child can keep his or her predictions.
- Work together each evening to forecast the next day's weather based on reports and intuition. Check your forecasts against the actual weather.
- Talk with your child about what a meteorologist does.

If your child has difficulty with the next pencil page, you can practice individual consonants by playing the "I'm going on a trip and I'm taking…" game, in which players alternately suggest items beginning or ending with a particular consonant.

Consonant Sounds

Name each picture and then write the missing letters. You can do it!

__oo__

__ago__

__io__

__i__

__ea__

__oa__

__ee__

__oo__

__o__

Look back at your weather words or weather rhymes.
What beginning and ending consonants did you use?

Picture Names: *door, wagon, lion, six, bear, goat, jeep, hook, mop*

11

Sky Watch

Have you checked out the sky today? Do you see any clouds? Are they puffy like cotton candy? Or long and wispy like a horse's tail? Clouds come in many shapes and sizes. They also have different names.

 ## Cirrus, Cumulus, Stratus

Let's take a look at three kinds of clouds:

1. **Cirrus** clouds appear highest in the sky. They're thin and feathery, like paint strokes.

2. **Cumulus** clouds are thick and puffy, like clumps of cotton balls or mounds of mashed potatoes.

3. **Stratus** clouds are low, flat clouds that spread across the sky like a quilt. Fog is a very low stratus cloud.

Create a collage of cloud pictures that you cut out from old magazines. Name and label the clouds. How many different cloud combinations did you find?

Cloud names can be combined to describe combination formations. *Cirrocumulus,* for example, names high cumulus clouds that resemble delicate "fish scales" (a mackerel sky). *Stratocumulus* names low, billowing cloud layers, and *cumulonimbus,* with *nimbus* meaning "rain," names dark, towering rain clouds.

 ## Cloud Gazing

The next time you're outside, look for cloud pictures. Use your imagination to find shapes and pictures in the clouds. Do you see an ice-cream cone? How about a rabbit or a dragon? What stories can you make up for these pictures? Try writing about one of your ideas!

Why Does It Rain?

Would you believe the sun makes it rain? Try this experiment to see why. You'll need a stove, so make sure a grownup helps.

- Ask a grownup to boil a pot of water. As the water heats, bubbles of air called water vapor rise up. When this vapor hits the cold air, it turns to steam.

- Have a grownup place a lid over the pot for a few seconds and then remove it. See how the steam that collected on the lid turned into tiny water droplets?

The sun is like a stove heating Earth's water. The water vapor from Earth turns into clouds when it hits the cold air. It begins to rain when the clouds can't hold any more moisture.

Here are two more ways to make clouds and rain:

- Exhale (breathe out) on a cold mirror or window. What happens when your warm breath hits the mirror?

- Take a cold soda can into a warm room. What happens to the outside of the can?

Rain Clouds

Some clouds carry rain. Discover which ones by listing the clouds you see when it rains. Try recording the daily rainfall by taping a ruler to the side of a clear jar to make a simple rain gauge.

At the end of the week, check your notes. What conclusions can you draw about the clouds you saw and the kind of weather they brought?

The following pencil page practices *l*, *r*, and *s* clusters. Weather words containing clusters include: *blizzard, breeze, clear, cloudy, crisp, dry, freezing, moist, sleet, slush, snow, storm,* and *sweltering.* As your child works through the chapter, look together for more cluster words.

Consonant Clusters

Name each picture and write the missing letters. Can you find two weather words?

____ar

____ow

____ouse

____oud

____oon

____ush

____etzel

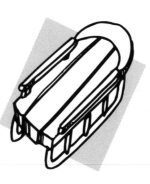

____ed

____ing

Picture Names: *star, cloud, snow, blouse, spoon, brush, pretzel, sled, swing*

Blow, Wind, Blow

What is all around you, but you can't see it? Air! When air moves, it's called wind. You can't see wind, but you can feel it. And, you can see the things it moves.

Make-Believe Tornado

Try watching a swirling tornado with this experiment. You'll need two large plastic soda bottles, some strong tape, and a grownup's help.

- Fill one bottle 1/3 of the way full with water.
- Place the empty bottle over the first bottle, neck to neck.
- Hold the bottle in place while a grownup securely tapes the bottle necks together.
- Hold the bottles by the necks. Turn them so that the bottle with the water is on top and rotate them quickly—as if you're stirring something.
- Stop rotating and watch. The swirling water should form a funnel, just like a tornado, as it runs into the empty bottle.

Wind Wheel

You can make a toy that moves with the wind. You'll need a six-inch square of paper, a pencil, scissors, and a straight pin.

- Draw two lines on the paper square, from corner to corner.
- Cut in three inches from each corner toward the center along the lines.
- Then bend every other corner to the center.
- Push a pin through the folded corners and the center. Ask a grownup to push the pin into the pencil. You've got a wind wheel!

Blow on your wind wheel to make it turn. What makes the wheel turn faster? Slower? Take your wind wheel outside. Hold it up and turn around slowly until it catches the wind. Can you tell from which direction the wind is blowing?

Make the tornado's funnel more pronounced by narrowing the opening in one bottle neck. Take a slice of potato and poke a hole in it. Place the neck of the bottle over the hole in the potato and push down. This cuts the potato, creating a disk that narrows the opening.

Sunny Days Are Here Again

Sunny days often lure people outdoors. Here are some recipes that combine the indoors and outdoors!

Sun Tea

Put the sun to work for you to make sun tea!

- Fill a large glass pitcher or jar with water.
- Place three or four tea bags into the water. You can also add some mint leaves, lemon, and sugar.
- Label your jar "Sun Tea."
- Put a lid on the pitcher and set it in the sun.
- In a few hours, you'll have sun tea. Pour it into glasses of ice and enjoy.

Flavored Snowballs

Even a snowy day can be sunny. After a snowfall, bring some clean new snow inside. Shape the snow into a ball and place it in a bowl. Drip maple syrup on top and eat as flavored ice!

Help Hungry Birds

Birds get hungry in the winter, but you can help. Try making one of these bird "feeders."

- Use a darning needle and some strong thread to string together popcorn, cranberries, or dried fruit. Drape the strings from tree branches and watch what happens.
- Coat a pine cone with a natural fruit preserve and sprinkle it with birdseed. Tie the pine cone to a tree branch and see who comes.

Help your child keep a record of the birds that visit the feeders. How many different kinds of birds visit? Does the weather affect when the birds visit?

The pencil page that follows practices the digraphs *ch, sh,* and *th,* as in the weather words <u>ch</u>illy, <u>sh</u>owers, <u>th</u>under, and wea<u>th</u>er.

Consonant Digraphs

Name each picture. Then write **ch**, **sh**, or **th** to complete the word.

_____ain

bru_____

_____imble

pea_____

_____air

pa_____

_____ip

_____umb

Picture Names: *chain, brush, thimble, peach, chair, path, ship, thumb*

Books to Share

The books suggested here are a sampling of fiction and nonfiction titles to help you and your child explore the weather.

Cloudy with a Chance of Meatballs by Judi Barrett (Aladdin, 1982). In the town of Chewandswallow, meals rain from the sky, but a change in the weather brings major problems for the residents.

Earth Weather, as Explained by Professor Xargle by Jeanne Willis (Dutton, 1993). In this spoof, Professor Xargle explains Earth's weather, and how Earthlets cope with it, to his extraterrestrial class.

Weatherwatch by Valerie Wyatt (Addison, 1990). For the budding scientist who would like more weather experiments and explanations, this is a good, readable choice.

Mike's Kite by Elizabeth MacDonald (Orchard, 1990). One day, Mike is flying his kite when a gust of wind sweeps him off his feet, and soon the whole town is trying to help him come down.

My Story Suggestions

Read aloud with your child the title on the next page. Then invite your child to read the story to you. After he or she reads the first two frames, pause together to predict what the contest might be and who might win. Then read on to check your predictions.

✱ This story is based on an Aesop fable whose moral is "Gentle persuasion will win where force fails." You and your child may enjoy creating another contest between the sun and the wind. What will the contest be? Who will win? Will your story have a lesson or moral?

More books you might enjoy:

Flannel Kisses by Linda Crotta Brenna (Houghton, 1997). The magic of a snowy day is captured in rhyming text and vibrant illustrations.

Lost in the Storm by Carol Carrick (Clarion, 1974). A young boy must wait out an island storm before being able to search for his lost dog.

Storms by Seymour Simon (Mulberry, 1992). Full-color photographs help children to examine thunderstorms, tornadoes, and hurricanes.

Weather Forecasting by Gail Gibbons (Aladdin, 1993). This behind-the-scenes look at a modern weather station simplifies a complex subject.

The Contest

1

North Wind and Sun were always quarreling about who was stronger.

2

"Let's have a contest," said Sun. "Yes, a contest," roared North Wind. "Then we'll see who is stronger."

3

"See that man?" said Sun. "Whoever can take the coat from his shoulders is stronger."
"Okay," roared North Wind. "It's a contest."

4

North Wind blew. He blew hard and cold. But the harder and colder North Wind blew, the tighter the man held onto his coat.

Now it was Sun's turn. Sun began to shine. Sun shone warmer and warmer rays. Soon the man was so hot that he took off the coat. Sun won the contest.

What do you think North Wind will say to Sun?
Draw and write about your ideas.

_____ .

Be Kind to the Earth

Hurt No Living Thing

Hurt no living thing;

Ladybird, nor butterfly,

Nor moth with dusty wing,

Nor cricket chirping cheerily,

Nor grasshopper so light of leap,

Nor dancing gnat, nor beetle fat,

Nor harmless worms that creep.

Christina Rossetti

Be Kind to the Earth

Recycling helps many children to realize that they can make a difference in the world, even through small actions. In *Be Kind to the Earth*, your child will have the chance to explore some of the ways he or she can make a difference while practicing these phonics and reading skills:

SHORT VOWELS: In first grade, children were introduced to the CVC (Consonant-Vowel-Consonant) spelling pattern that signals a word with a short vowel sound. In this chapter, your child will review and practice reading words that follow this pattern.

LONG VOWELS: Children are usually introduced to long vowel sounds through CVC*e* (Consonant-Vowel-Consonant-*e*) words, such as *tape, bike, joke,* and *cute.* CVC*e* words are also reviewed here.

COMPOUND WORDS: Young readers often find long words daunting, and they are especially proud when they can decode and read compound words. Here, your child will practice looking for the two words that make up a compound word.

COMPARE/CONTRAST: One way in which children learn is to compare and contrast items. In second grade, children go beyond simple comparison and contrast of physical traits, such as color, size, and shape; they begin to compare and contrast more abstract concepts, such as experiment results or the past and the present.

CATEGORIZE/CLASSIFY: Children continue to practice and use this important thinking skill and begin to learn more about its application in real life. Sorting objects for recycling is a perfect example of how we categorize and classify.

The reading strategy mentioned in Chapter 1 was making predictions. A second reading strategy children use is *monitoring.* This strategy involves determining whether the text in a story or article makes sense and what to do if it doesn't. If something doesn't make sense, readers are taught to apply "fix-up" strategies such as:

- reading again for information;
- reading ahead for information;
- looking at illustrations for help.

Home, Sweet Home

Think about your home. What would happen if you let dirty clothes and trash and dust build up? You'd have quite a mess, right? Well, Earth is also your home. What can you do to help protect it and keep it clean?

Friends-of-Earth

With your family, make a list of things you can do together to help Earth. Think about things that help save natural resources. such as energy, water, and trees. Then talk about your list. Which things can you start doing right away? Which need more planning?

Family Recycling

If your town is like most towns, it probably has a recycling program. That's where people save and sort items like newspapers, glass, plastic, and cans to be taken to a recycling center. Instead of going to a dump or a landfill, the collected items are made into things people can use again. In fact, that's what **recycle** means—**to use again.**

If you don't have a recycling plan in your home, now is a good time to start one. Get several plastic bins or garbage cans to hold recyclables. Label the bins to make sorting easier. After a week, take a look at the "trash" you've collected. Aren't you glad these items won't be cluttering your Earth home?

Plan a visit to a town or commercial recycling center. Kids will be amazed by how much would be wasted if it weren't recycled.

Recycling is mandated in most towns. Your city council or town hall can provide details specific to your local program.

Don't Be a Litterbug

Do litterbugs bug you? Then bug some friends to help you pick up the litter around your school or neighborhood. You can also try these activities.

"Don't Litter" Sign

Make a "don't litter" sign for a neighborhood trash can.

- Plan your sign. What do you want to say about littering? Think of a catchy phrase or rhyme to get people's attention. Jot down your ideas.

- Use construction paper or poster board and bright crayons or markers for your sign.

- Add pictures to help get your message across. But keep the sign simple and clear.

- Hang your sign where others will see it.

Litter Bags

Why do so many people throw litter from cars? Maybe it's because they don't have a place to "stash their trash." Try making a litter bag for your car. With a black marker, write "Don't Litter" on the front of a paper bag. Then decorate it. Hang the bag from the back of a seat.

Help organize a group cleanup of the school grounds, a park, or a stream. Create a flyer to advertise the event. (Check with local authorities beforehand.)

The following pencil page practices the CVC short vowel pattern. After your child completes the page, invite him or her to see which words can be "recycled." Suggest another vowel that can be placed between each set of consonants. For example, a *u* turns *fan* and *fin* into *fun*.

Short Vowels

Circle the word that names each picture.

fan fin

bag bug

tack tuck

pet pot

not nut

pin pan

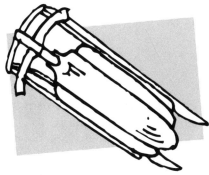

sled slid

jot jet

Be Tree Friendly

Trees are an important natural resource. Wood from trees is used to build furniture and homes. Did you know it's also used to make paper? In fact, one tree per person is used each year just for paper. That means a family of four uses four trees a year! So how can you be a friend to trees? Read on.

Save a Tree

Begin a list of the paper products your family uses. Then try to think of a way you might recycle or reuse each item. You might turn paper grocery bags into book covers, or use the Sunday comics to wrap a present. These questions should give you a couple more ideas:

- What can I do with wrapping paper from gifts?

- How many times can I reuse my paper lunch bag?

Recycle Paper

You know recycling newspapers helps to save trees. But what about paper from schoolwork, notebooks, and mail? Did you know that you can recycle that paper, too?

Decorate a box and label it "Recycled Paper." Use the box to store old school work, notebook pages, and other papers. Then, the next time you need to make a list or play Tic-Tac-Toe, use the back of your recycled paper instead of a clean sheet.

 Washable canvas bags and string bags make excellent reusable shopping bags. To purchase a canvas bag with the "Save a Tree" logo, write to:
Save a Tree
P.O. Box 862
Berkeley, CA 94701

 The following pencil page practices the CVC*e* long vowel spelling pattern.

Long Vowels

Circle the word that names each picture.

mule   mile

tap   tape

goat   gate

cute   cut

bake   bike

rob   robe

bone   box

pine   pin

Water Wise

How do you use water? For drinking? Brushing your teeth? Washing your clothes? Everyone uses water. Try these experiments to see how much water you really use around the house.

🕐 Brush Your Teeth

Can you save water when you brush your teeth? Try this to find out:

- Shut the drain in the sink. Then turn on the water. Leave the water running as you wet your toothbrush, brush your teeth, and rinse. Notice how much water is in the sink.

- Then drain the sink and start the experiment again. This time, wet your toothbrush and turn off the water while you brush. Turn the water back on to rinse. Which way saves water?

🕐 Bath Time

Which uses more water—a shower or a bath? Try this to find out.

- The next time you take a bath, measure how deep the water is with a ruler. The next time, take a shower. Be sure to close the drain so you can see how much water you use. Did you use more water taking a shower or a bath?

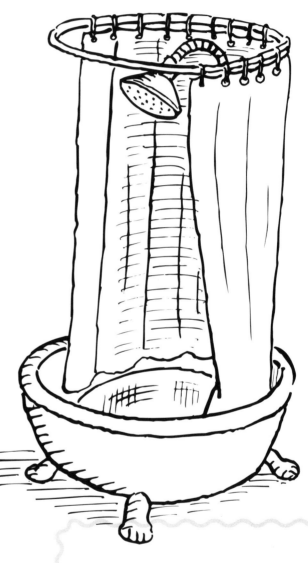

The average sink holds one gallon of water. A tub holds 40 gallons.

The following pencil page practices compound words. If necessary, remind your child that a compound word is made up of two shorter words. Help your child list compounds with *water*, such as *waterfall, watermelon, dishwater,* and *rainwater.*

Compound Words

Write the word that names each picture. Draw a line between the two small words that make up each compound.

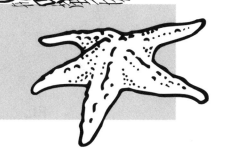

horseshoe
houseboat

horse/shoe

clotheshorse
clothesline

_____

sandpaper
starfish

_____

fireplace
firefighter

_____

seashell
eggshell

_____

backpack
barefoot

_____

All Creatures

Earth is your home. It is also home to many different creatures. Some of these creatures are endangered. This means that their total population keeps getting smaller. Just like dinosaurs, these animals are in danger of becoming extinct.

Some Endangered Animals

Bald Eagle

Desert Tortoise

Blue Whale

Manatee

Brown Bear

Gray Wolf

California Condor

Prairie Dog

 ## Save an Animal

There are many reasons animals become endangered. Some have no place to live because their homes are destroyed. Some are hunted. Some are poisoned by chemicals in the water and ground. Which endangered animal would you like to learn more about? Check out a library book about that animal.

Make a poster that tells about your animal. On your poster, you can draw and write to tell:

- what the animal looks like,
- what it eats,
- where it lives,
- why it is endangered,
- what people can do to help.

- Many nature stores and catalogs sell endangered animal adoption kits. Your child can receive pictures and newsletters updating the progress of your animal.
- Help your child go on line to get more information about an endangered animal, if you have access to the Internet.

Wrapping Up

You've come to the end of the chapter, but not to the end of things you can do to help protect and clean up Earth! The most important thing is to try to reuse and to recycle everything you can. Here are two more activities to send you on your way.

Recycled Words

How do you recycle a word? Change the first letter to create a new word! You can do this with a sliding word card. Here's how to make one, using the word **can**:

- Write the word **can** on an index card. Cut an inch-long slit above and below the letter **c**.

- Next, cut out a strip of paper. Write different consonant letters down the strip.

- Pass the letter strip through the slits on the word card.

- As a letter appears in the window, read the new word.

Kitchen Ecology

Ask a grownup to help you explore the kitchen cabinets for different kinds of food. Can you find products packaged in boxes made from recycled paper?

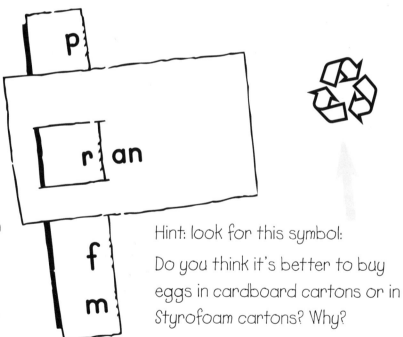

Hint: look for this symbol:

Do you think it's better to buy eggs in cardboard cartons or in Styrofoam cartons? Why?

This chapter's activities help children "see" the results of their actions. See the "Books to Share" list on the next page for more Earth-friendly ideas.

Books to Share

The books here offer a range of material available with information on our environment.

The Great Kapok Tree by Lynn Cherry (Harcourt, 1990). As a tree cutter takes a nap beneath a great kapok tree in the Brazilian rain forest, the animals in the tree beg him not to destroy their world.

Deep Down Underground by Olivier Dunrea (Aladdin, 1993). When a mole goes digging, his movements set off a ripple effect among the worms, frogs, spiders, and other underground dwellers.

The Earth and I by Frank Asch (Gulliver, 1994). A story about a friendship that one child has with the earth.

A River Ran Wild by Lynn Cherry (Harcourt, 1992). This easy-to-read book, tells of the successful clean-up of New England's once-polluted Nashua River.

More books you might enjoy:

The Lorax by Dr. Seuss (Random, 1971). What happens to the Lorax when all the trees are cut down for a factory? Find out in this Dr. Seuss classic.

V for Vanishing: An Alphabet of Endangered Animals by Patricia Mullens (Harper, 1994). From the armadillo to the zebra, children learn about the plight of different endangered animals.

The Big Book for Our Planet edited by Ann Durell, Jean Craighead George, and Katherine Paterson (Dutton, 1993). A collection of poems, stories, and artwork on environmental protection.

Earth Book for Kids by Linda Schwartz (Learning Works, 1990). Through activities and projects, children and families learn about the environment while having fun.

Suggestions

Read aloud the title on the next page with your child. Then invite him or her to read the story to you. After your child reads each frame, ask him or her if it makes sense. Encourage your child to tell how Mother Kangaroo and Joey are being friendly to Earth.

✱ You and your child may enjoy creating your own Earth-friendly "do and don't" list for your next shopping trip.

Earth Friendly

"Let's be Earth friendly and walk," said Joey. "Cars pollute the air."

"This is good exercise," said Mother.
"It's fun," said Joey. "And we're saving gas, too."

"We don't need a bag, Joey," said Mom. "Bananas come in their own packaging."
"Good idea, Mom," said Joey.

"Let's get eggs in a cardboard carton," said Joey. "We can't recycle that other stuff."
"Good thinking," said Mom.

"Paper or plastic?" asked the clerk.
"Neither," said Joey. "We're Earth friendly. We brought a pouch."

What can you do to be Earth friendly at the grocery store?
Draw and write about your ideas.

_____ .

All Around the Town

The Key to the Kingdom

This is the key to the kingdom:

In that kingdom is a city,

In that city is a town,

In that town there is a street,

In that street there winds a lane,

In that lane there is a yard,

In that yard there is a house,

In that house there is a room,

In that room there is a bed,

On that bed there is a basket,

A basket of flowers.

Traditional

All Around the Town

Most second graders have an understanding of what a community is and how people within a community interact. In this chapter, your child will have a chance to take a closer look at his or her own community and learn more about the people, places, and things it has to offer, while practicing these reading skills:

VOWEL PAIRS: Children continue learning about vowel sounds and spellings as they explore vowel pairs. In this chapter, they'll practice the vowel sounds for *ai* as in *rain, ay* as in *ray, ee* as in *jeep, ea* as in *bead* and *bread, oa* as in *boat, ou* as in *loud,* and *ow* as in *owl* and *low.*

MAKING GENERALIZATIONS: People make generalizations based on their prior experiences. Your child is learning to make generalizations based on his or her experiences as well. Encourage your child to learn more to confirm or change a generalization.

MAKING JUDGMENTS: As children learn more about their surroundings, they begin to look at them with a critical eye. As you work together to complete an activity in this chapter, encourage your child to make judgments about the things he or she learns. What can be done to make a place better? Why should a particular building be saved? Torn down?

Children are also learning to make judgments as they read. This reading strategy is called *evaluating.* During and after reading with your child, you might ask questions such as the following:

- Did you like the story? Why or why not?
- Did the book answer your questions?
- Did you learn anything new? What was it?

My Town Is...

Is your town big or small? Is it old or new? Are there lots of buildings or just a few? What do you like best about your town?

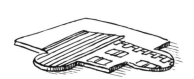

"My Town" Puzzle

Draw a picture to show what you like best about your town and put a label under it. Now, turn your picture into a jigsaw puzzle. Here's how:

- Glue the drawing to heavy paper or cardboard.
- After the glue dries, turn the drawing over.
- Draw puzzle shapes on the back of the drawing. Then ask a grownup to cut out the pieces.

Invite a family member to guess what you like best about your town. Let that person put the puzzle together to see if he or she guessed correctly.

Town Folder

Talk about your town with a family member and discuss places you've visited or want to visit.

Learn more about your town. Look for photographs and articles in newspapers or magazines. Cut out the things you find or write down what you learn. Is there anything you learned that surprised you?

Save the information in a folder. You can add to your collection as you learn more about your town.

Enlist the aid of your local librarian to research your town's history. Or, visit the town hall, the fire department, or the police station to obtain information.

Your child might use a binder to begin a scrapbook of the information he or she collects.

Up the Road

What connects the school to your house? The library to the grocery store? Did you guess roads? Roads help bring a town together. They help connect people, places, and things.

Be a Town Detective

Take a walk with a grownup along a road in your town. It could be a main street with many stores, or it could be the road you live on. Take a notebook so you can list everything you see. Include buildings, homes, side streets, and landmarks like parks, bus stops, and trees.

Cut open a paper grocery bag to provide a large surface for the map. Your child can also create a giant "patch-work" map by taping on additional maps of other neighborhoods.

Map It

Share what you found on your walk by drawing a map. Your list can help you remember all you saw. Start by drawing a double line to show the road. Then add places and things. These ideas can help you:

- Use a pencil so you can make changes easily.

- Show houses and buildings with squares and rectangles.

- Try different shapes for other things, like circles for trees and bushes or triangles for parks.

- Label the places you put on the map. Ask a grownup how to spell something if you need help.

- When your map is complete, trace over it with a black marker and color it in.

Vowel Pairs: ai, ay

Find the hidden picture name and circle it. Write the circled words at the bottom of the page in the correct column.

daday(daisy)

passprayai

papaypail

aytrayrainy

rtrainrain

manmailmay

ai words

daisy

_____

_____

_____

ay words

_____

_____

_____

Picture Names: *daisy, spray, pay, tray, train, mail*

39

Read All About It

Where's the best place to find out about what's going on in your town? The newspaper, of course. Let's take a look.

⏱ News Know-How

When you look through a newspaper, you'll usually find the most important news stories on the front page. But a newspaper has all kinds of information. Look through a newspaper with a grownup. How many headlines can you read? How many of these features can you find?

news story

sports story

comics

store ads

up-coming events

weather

✋ Help your child create a more professional looking newspaper by using a computer word processing program. Many programs have newsletter templates with two- and three-column formats.

💡 Your child and a small group of friends can work together to create a neighborhood newspaper. Each child can contribute a story and a feature. Photocopy the end result so each child has a paper.

☁ Your Own Newspaper

What's it like to work on a newspaper? You can find out by making your own! Write about an exciting thing that happened during the week. Draw some generalizations. Ask friends or family members for news, too. You can report their news in your paper, or invite them to write a news story for you.

Write your stories neatly or ask a grownup to help you. Give each story a headline. Draw a few pictures, too. You might even include a comic strip.

Finally, give your paper a name. Write it in big letters across the top of the front page. Make copies for family and friends.

Vowel Pairs: ee, ea

Name the pictures. Then write the words by the matching numbers to complete the puzzle. What vowel sounds do you hear?

beak
sweater
bead
sheep
seat
bee
bread
steam

ACROSS

1.

3.

5.

6.

DOWN

1.

2.

3.

4.

Picture Names: *seat, sweater, bee, bead, steam, bread, sheep, beak*

41

Who's Who?

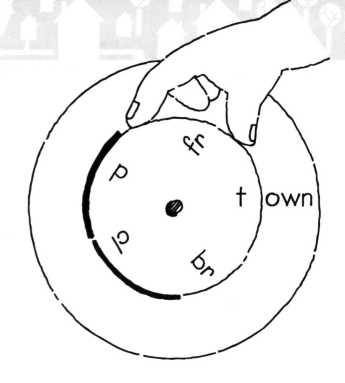

How do people in your town help you? Think about the workers in your town and their jobs. Family members, teachers, mail carriers, firefighters, police officers, doctors, nurses. Who else helps you?

 Job Interview

Is there someone in town who has a job you would like to know more about? Ask a grownup to help you write a note to this person. Your note should include this information:

- Your name.
- What you'd like to learn about the person's job.
- The name of your grownup helper, so this person can call your helper.
- A thank-you sentence and your signature.

Around Town

What else is happening "around town"? Make a word wheel for **town** to find out.

1) Get two paper plates. Cut the rim off one plate so you have a big circle and a small circle.

2) Print **own** on the edge of the big circle.

3) Print the letters **t, br, cl, d,** and **fr** around the edge of the small circle.

4) Attach the small circle to the big circle with a paper fastener.

5) Turn the small circle to read the words.

Now make a word wheel for **show**. Write the letters **sh, bl, gr, sl,** and **st** on the small circle.

Vowel Pairs: oa, ow, ou

Who hides in the town grass? To find out, color green the words with the vowel sound in **road**. Then color brown the words with the vowel sound in **town**.

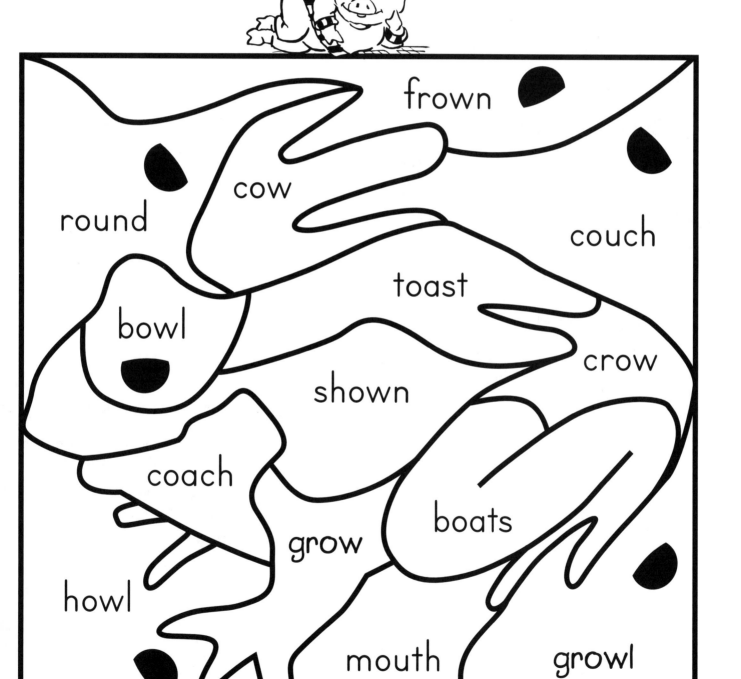

frown

cow

round

couch

bowl

toast

crow

shown

coach

boats

grow

howl

mouth

growl

43

Food for Thought

Where in your town can you get food? At the grocery store? A bakery? How about a deli or a restaurant? How about your own kitchen?

Creamy Fruit Cup

Looking for a breakfast treat? Or maybe a cool snack? Try this creamy fruit cup. It's sure to surprise everyone in the family. First, gather these ingredients:

> 1 can of mandarin orange sections
>
> 1 can of pineapple chunks
>
> 1 cup of red or green seedless grapes
>
> 1 8-ounce carton of plain yogurt

With a grownup's help, open and drain the cans of fruit and put them into a mixing bowl. Add the grapes and the yogurt. Then gently stir the fruit until it is coated with the yogurt. Spoon the fruit into small bowls. Enjoy!

Try making this creamy fruit cup with strawberries and blueberries for a red, white, and blue dessert!

Gelatin Singles

Ask a grownup to help you make your favorite gelatin. Add mini marshmallows, nuts, or banana slices, if you'd like. Pour the gelatin into small paper cups and refrigerate. The next time you want a snack, reach for a cup!

With your child, list the places in town or around your neighborhood where people can get food. Talk about where the foods come from and all the workers involved in getting the foods to the store.

The following pencil page practices contractions. If necessary, remind your child that some pairs of words can be written or said as a contraction: two words written as one with an apostrophe that takes the place of one or more letters. Give examples such as *did not* and *didn't*. Ask your child to help you find contractions when reading.

Contractions

Read the letter. Write each underlined pair of words as a contraction below.

April 1, 1998

Dear Carla,

    I am so sorry you could not visit this week. But next month will be even better. It is our town's 100th birthday, and we are having a big celebration. My parents will take us to the parade. Then we will go to a huge picnic and see some fireworks.

    You are sure to have a good time. So please say yes and do not say no.

            Your friend,

            Andy

P.S. Mom says she will come get you if you need a ride!

I'm _____   _____

_____   _____

_____   _____

_____   _____

Around the Town Game

Do you like board games? Well, here's a chance to create a board game that's all about your town.

 ## Create the Game Board

Gather together a large sheet of poster board, markers, index cards, and paper. Design a path for your game. Your path might be **S**-shaped or square like this one.

In each space, draw a picture of a place in your town and label it. Make sure you include your home. After all, the person to get HOME first wins!

After you finish the game board, make the game cards. On each card write a different instruction for the players. Make up at least ten different cards. Here are a few ideas:

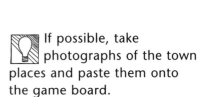

- Thank you for not littering. Go forward two.
- Feed the pigeons in the park. Miss one turn.
- Return a library book. Go forward one.

Practice playing the game with a family member.
- Do you need any special rules to play?
- Do you need more "go forward" or "go back" cards?
- Should people tell about a place when they land on it?

After you make your cards, invite the whole family to play!

If possible, take photographs of the town places and paste them onto the game board.

Looking for a fun way to review phonics skills or sight vocabulary? Try substituting the game cards with flash cards. For each correct response, a player advances a space.

Look at all the things I can do!

☐ I can read words I don't recognize by thinking about:

    ☐ beginning and ending consonant sounds.

    ☐ consonant groups with l, r, and s.

    ☐ the sounds ch, sh, and th.

    ☐ short vowel sounds.

    ☐ long vowel sounds.

    ☐ the vowel pairs ai, ay, ee, ea, oa, ow and ou.

    ☐ compound words.

☐ I can sort things and group them together in different ways.

☐ I can can look for details in stories to help me draw conclusions.

☐ I can compare and contrast things.

☐ I can make judgments about the things I read and see.

Books to Share

Many books have town and city settings. Listed here are just a few. As you and your child read together, compare and contrast the settings in the stories to your town.

Jamaica Louise James by Amy Hest (Candlewick, 1996). Jamaica uses the paints she receives for her birthday to create a special surprise for Grammy.

The Little House by Virginia Lee Burton (Houghton, 1942). This award-winning classic tells how a town and then a city grow up around a little house in the country.

Pearl Moscowitz's Last Stand by Arthur Levine (Tambourine, 1993). Over the years, Pearl has watched the trees her mother planted along their city street fall one by one. Now the very last one is about to be cut down, but Pearl has a plan to save it.

The Town Mouse and the Country Mouse by Janet Stevens (Holiday, 1987). Watercolors and an updated retelling bring this Aesop favorite into the twentieth century.

Suggestions

Invite your child to read the story on the next page to you. Help your child evaluate the story. Ask: Did you like this story? Why or why not? How important do you think Mike's job is?

✱ Invite your child to create a story around his or her favorite community neighbor or worker. Then discuss with your child why she or he picked that person.

More books you might enjoy:

The Night Ones by Patricia Grossman (Harcourt, 1991). Text and pictures provide information about many night workers needed in a city.

City Noise by Karla Kuskin (Harper, 1994). A little girl holds a tin can to her ear, like a conch shell, and hears an urban symphony.

Left Behind by Carol and Donald Carrick (Clarion, 1988). Christopher is accidentally left behind during a class trip.

Molasses Flood by Blair Lent (Houghton, 1987). On a warm January day, an explosion sends a flood of molasses through the streets of Boston.

Messenger Mike

Messenger Mike is always busy. The whole town needs him.

"Mike, please take this ice cream to Pat Cat," said Rabbit. "And please hurry. She's having a party."

"Mike, please take this cake to Pat Cat," said Bear. "And please hurry. She's having a party."

"Dear Mike. Please take these balloons to Pat Cat," said Fox's note. "And hurry. She's having a party."

"Surprise!" shouted Rabbit, Bear, Fox, and Pat Cat. "Thanks for all your hard work."

If you could throw a party for someone in your town, who would it be? Draw and write about your ideas.

_____.

The Moon and the Stars

The Star

Twinkle, twinkle, little star,
How I wonder what you are!
Up above the world so high,
Like a diamond in the sky.

When the blazing sun is gone,
When he nothing shines upon,
Then you show your little light,
Twinkle, twinkle, all the night.

Jane Taylor

A Note About The Moon and the Stars

The sun, moon, stars, and planets have always fascinated people. Long before scientists looked for answers, myths and legends evolved to explain the presence of these heavenly bodies. While exploring the moon and the stars in this chapter, your child will also practice these reading skills:

VOWEL PAIRS: Your child will continue to learn about vowel sounds as he or she practices these vowel pairs: *oo* as in *book* and *room, ew* as in *news,* and *ue* as in *blue.*

R- AND L-CONTROLLED VOWELS: As children explore vowels, they learn that some consonants can affect the sound of a vowel. The *a* in *talk,* for instance, is neither short (*tack*) nor long (*take*). The same is true for the *a* in *cart.* Your child will practice r- and l-controlled vowels here.

PREFIXES: In order to read unfamiliar words, second graders look for base words and then look for any endings, prefixes, and/or suffixes that have been attached to the words. Here, your child will practice reading words with the prefixes *re-, dis-,* and *un-.*

CATEGORIZE/CLASSIFY: In *The Moon and the Stars,* your child will continue to practice categorizing and classifying skills.

SEQUENCE: While reading, children practice sequence in terms of events that happen first, next, and last. In this chapter, your child will practice sequence to order planets, follow steps in a process, and write his or her own stories.

One important reading strategy children use is integrated word analysis or, more simply, they *think about words*. Here, children use several approaches to help them figure out an unfamiliar word, such as:
- thinking about the beginning letter(s) and sound(s) to decode the word;
- looking for familiar word parts (word families, compound words, endings, prefixes, and suffixes) to decode the word;
- thinking about the word to see if it makes sense in the sentence;
- looking at illustrations for clues to word meaning.

The Sun Is a Star

You know the sun gives us light and heat. And you probably know it helps plants and trees to grow. But did you know the sun is a star? It's true. It only seems large and bright because it's so close to Earth.

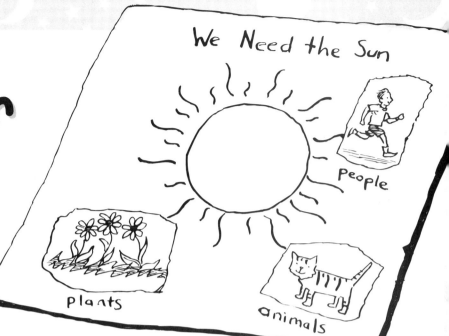

Day and Night

Have you ever seen a sunrise? How about a sunset? Now, think about this: The sun does not rise and the sun does not set. A globe (or a large ball) and a flashlight will help show what really happens.

- Point to where you live on the globe.

- Darken the room and shine a flashlight on the globe. The flashlight is like the sun. The lit side of the globe is having day. The dark side is having night.

- Slowly turn the globe. Earth rotates, or turns, every 24 hours. As parts of Earth turn into the sun, the sun **looks** as if it's rising. As parts of Earth turn away from the sun, the sun looks as if it's setting. But it's Earth that moves.

Sun Collage

Of all the things you see in the sky, the sun is the most important to life on Earth. Create a collage to show how living things need the sun.

- First, draw a picture of the sun.

- Then, around the sun, place pictures that show how Earth needs each thing. You can draw the pictures or cut them out from magazines.

- Title your collage or label the pictures to tell what they show.

Instead of using a globe, you can conduct the day and night experiment using a large ball and a flashlight. If so, use a marker or piece of tape to indicate a spot on the ball where you "live."

As your child works on the collage, help him or her to categorize and classify the pictures used.

It's Just a Phase

Have you ever seen a full moon? What about a half moon or a crescent moon? Why does the moon seem to change? Let's find out.

🕐 The Changing Moon

About once a month, the moon revolves, or travels, around Earth. This makes the moon **seem** to change. An unshaded lamp and a pencil poked into a tennis ball can help you see what really happens.

- Imagine that you are Earth. The tennis ball is the moon, and the lamp is the sun.

- Face the "sun." Hold the "moon" up and out in front of you. Does any sunlight hit the side of the moon you can see? No, the side of the moon you can see is dark. This is called a new moon.

- Now turn your whole body slowly to the left. The moon's lit side begins to show. At first, it looks like a crescent, or a fingernail. As you continue to turn, it becomes a half moon.

- When your back is to the sun, all the moon's lit side shows. This is a full moon. (Remember to hold the "moon" up so your body doesn't block the light!)

- Continue turning. What happens? Yes, less and less of the moon shows until you see another half moon, crescent moon, and new moon.

The moon didn't really change shape. The only thing that changed was the part that was lit.

🕐 Chart the Moon

With a grownup, check the moon each night. Record the date and draw a picture of what you see. How many days does it take for the moon to go through all its phases?

While recording the moon's phases, your child may notice that the second crescent and half moons face a different direction. If your child is confused by this, repeat the experiment for an explanation.

Compare your child's moon drawings to those that appear in the newspaper or on a calendar.

The pencil page that follows practices the vowel pairs *ew, ue,* and *oo.* After your child completes the page, ask him or her to name the kinds of moons shown.

Vowel Pairs: ew, ue oo

Find the hidden pictures. Color yellow the words with the vowel sound in **moon.** Color blue the words with the vowel sound in **good.**

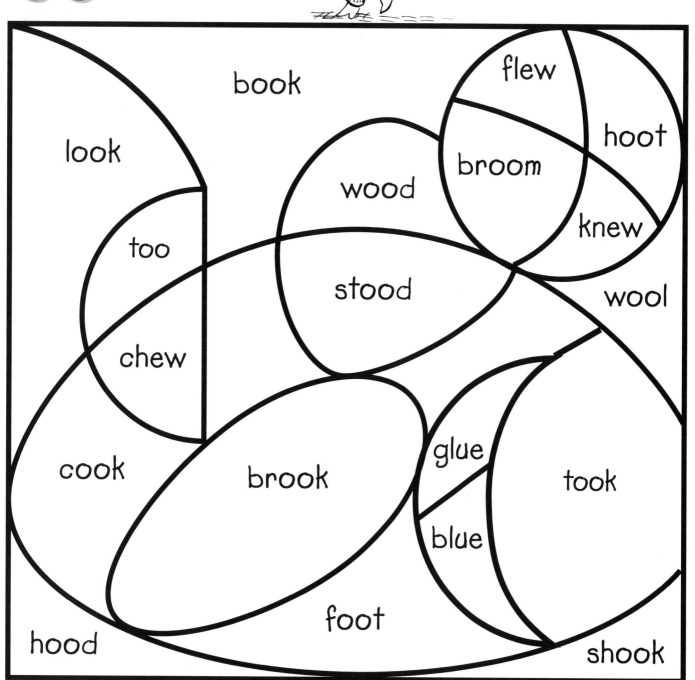

book

look

flew

hoot

broom

wood

too

stood

knew

chew

wool

cook

brook

glue

took

blue

foot

hood

shook

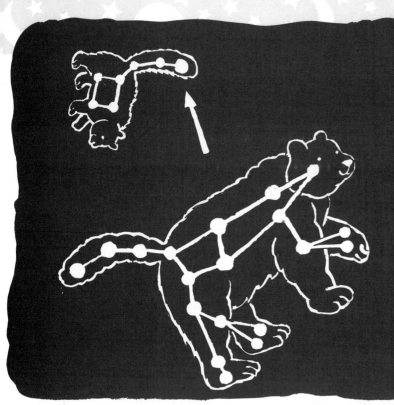

Star Stories

What do you see in the night sky? The moon? The stars? Groups of stars are called constellations. Long ago, people noticed these star groups night after night and made up stories about them.

🕐 The Big and Little Dippers

Two constellations people saw were the Big Dipper and the Little Dipper. Some people saw a big and a little bear when they looked at the star groups.

According to one legend, a woman and her son were so wicked and mean that they were turned into bears. Each bear was then grabbed by its short tail and swung round and round until the tail became very long. Then the bears were hurled far into the night sky where they still spin around the North Star.

Do you see bears when you look at the Big and Little Dippers? Do you see something else? What story would you tell about them?

🕐 Create a Constellation

You can make "constellations" using paper cups and a flashlight. On the bottom of a paper cup, poke holes with a pencil to make a pattern. Then put the cup over the flashlight and turn out the lights. Turn on the flashlight and aim it at the ceiling to enjoy your constellation!

Take a closer look at your constellation. What shapes do you see? Do you see an animal or a person? Something else?

Find the Big Dipper's bowl in the bear. The two stars on the right side point to the North Star. With your child, look for the Big and Little Dippers on a clear night. Can you find the North Star?

Use books or star charts to help you find the constellations in the night sky.

Vowels with r

A word that has a vowel followed by an **r** is hiding in the letters beside each number. Circle the word and print it in the boxes. The clues can help you.

1) (THIRD)FIRS

Earth's order in the planets

2) M O R S T A R O N

Something in the night sky

3) V E R B H A R T X

An action word

4) F I R S T O M R E

Mercury's order in the planets

5) O C H U R L F A R

To throw with force

6) R D A R K H E A V

The opposite of **light**

7) I S O R H M A R S

The fourth planet from the sun

8) O U T U R N F N E

To rotate or revolve

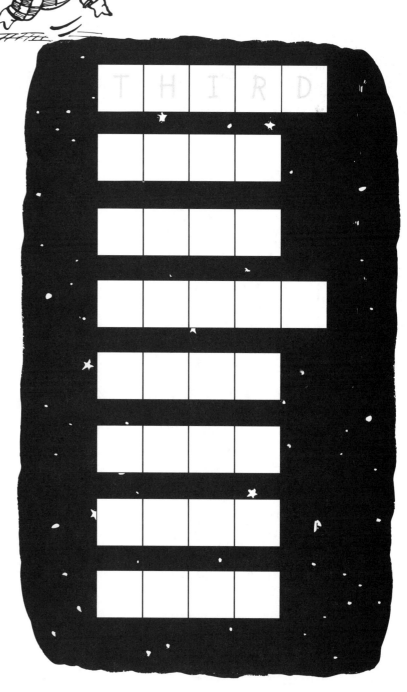

| T | H | I | R | D |

Moon Magic

 Just as people told stories about the stars, they made up stories about the moon. Maybe you've heard about the man in the moon or the moon's being made of Swiss cheese. We know these stories aren't true. But they're still fun—like these moon creations.

Moon Pies

Place a small scoop of soft vanilla ice cream between two chocolate chip cookies. Gently press the cookies together to make a moon pie. Make enough pies for your whole family. Then store each one in a plastic bag and put them in the freezer. When the ice cream refreezes, they're ready to eat!

Toothpicks can be used in place of pretzel sticks and gum drops in place of marshmallows.

After your child finishes the following pencil page, encourage him or her to use the words in sentences.

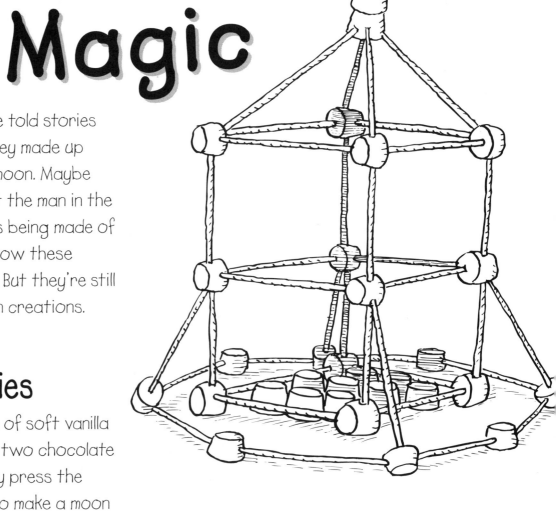

Moon Station

You can create a crazy moon station. All you need are some marshmallows and some thin pretzel sticks.

- To begin, stick a marshmallow onto each end of a thin pretzel stick. Repeat this until you have several "marshmallow barbells."
- Build your moon station by using more pretzel sticks to join the barbells together.

Invite some friends over to help you eat the moon station. Brainstorm ideas for a story that might take place on the station.

Prefixes

disagree

respell   redo

reappear

repay

disappear

undone

unwrap

Read the words in the box and then read the clues. Write the words by the matching numbers to finish the puzzle.

ACROSS

3. not done

5. to appear again

6. to do again

7. to pay back

DOWN

1. not agree

2. to spell again

3. to do the opposite of wrap

4. to do the opposite of appear

What two words might you use to describe what the moon seems to do at different times of the month?

Nine Planets

Earth is not a moon or a star. It's a planet that travels around the sun. There are eight more planets. Can you name them?

Planet Memories

The nine planets, in order from the sun, are: Mercury, Venus, Earth, Mars, Jupiter, Saturn, Uranus, Neptune, and Pluto.

Some people use sentences to help them remember the planets in order. Can you figure out how these sentences help? (Hint: Look at the first letter of each word.)

- **M**y **v**ery **e**ager **m**onkey **j**ust **s**campered **u**p **n**ine **p**oles.

- **M**om **v**acuumed **e**arly **M**onday. **J**ust **s**traighten **u**p **n**ow, **p**lease.

Ask a grownup to help you make up your own sentence to remember the names and order of the planets.

Planet Mobile

Make a mobile of the planets! You'll need construction paper, string, and a hanger. Here are some ideas for making your mobile:

- Use paper circles of different sizes to show the planets and a yellow circle for the sun.

- Label the sun and each planet.

- Plan how to arrange your planets. Will you hang them in planet order? Or, will you group them by size?

- Attach each planet to the hanger with a string.

Your child can use cups or bowls of different sizes to trace circles for the planets. Encourage your child to learn more about the planets and to add special features to the mobile, such as the rings around Saturn.

Vowels with l

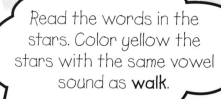

bad

talk

salt

ball

fall

bald

thank

sail

small

chalk

chain

smile

Answers: *talk, salt, ball, fall, bald, small, chalk*

In the News

We are learning more about the moon, the stars, and the planets every day. Keep up with the news to find out more!

In the News

The most important news of the day appears on the front page of a newspaper. When astronauts landed on the moon, it was front page news. And, it'll be front page news when the first astronauts land on Mars. For now, most news about the moon, the stars, and the planets is found in science magazines or in the science section of newspapers.

Ask a grownup to help you find an "in the news" article. Read the article together and talk about it. What questions does the article answer? What new questions does it bring to mind?

Internet web sites can keep you abreast of newsworthy events, such as the one set up to cover the Mars landing in 1997. If you have access to the Internet, your child can search the web for the latest space news. You might also visit the NASA web site where you can connect to a "kids" section that answers common questions and offers pictures, articles, and features.

Did You Know?

For a long time, scientists believed there were only eight planets. That's because Pluto was too small and too far away to be seen, even with a telescope. But as telescopes and other equipment became more advanced, people began to suspect that there was a ninth planet! Finally, in 1930, a scientist named Clyde Tombaugh discovered and named Pluto.

Are there more planets in our solar system? Could be. In fact, you might be the scientist to discover the next planet. Think about it! Then write a news story to tell about your discovery. You might include information such as:

- size and appearance of the planet;
- what you named it and why;
- number of moons, if any.

Out of This World

Spaceships? Little green men from Mars? Stories about make-believe creatures and space events are called science fiction. Can you think of any science fiction TV shows or movies you've seen? Try your hand at being a science-fiction writer!

 ## My Own Story

Before you begin your story, brainstorm a few ideas. Ask yourself questions like these:

- What part of my story will be real? What part will be make-believe?

- Will the story take place on the moon? On a planet?

- What kind of space creatures will I include? Will they be friendly or unfriendly?

Once you have your ideas, write a rough draft of your story. Share it with a grownup. Are there parts you want to change? How can you make the story better?

Write your finished story neatly. Draw pictures to go with it.

Create a Model

Design a model for a space vehicle or a creature in your story. You can use a plastic soda bottle for the body along with these ideas:

- Cut out shapes from colored paper for your creature's eyes, noses, and mouths.

- Cut out and fold up thin cardboard strips for arms and/or antennae.

- Add buttons for knobs or dials.

- Use other supplies or decorations, such as pipe cleaners, aluminum foil, or cotton balls.

A writer often brainstorms ideas, writes a rough draft, and shares the draft for ideas. After proofreading and editing the draft, he or she publishes the work by producing a finished copy. Encourage your child to use these steps as he or she writes a science-fiction story.

Books to Share

Many second graders want facts, and that's just what you'll find in the books listed here.

Earth, Sky, and Beyond by Jean-Pierre Verdet (Lodestar, 1995). This nonfiction title offers an introductory journey into space to learn about the moon, the sun, and all nine planets.

Find the Constellations by H.A. Rey (Houghton, 1976). The creator of the Curious George books presents an informative beginner's guide to locating and identifying constellations.

Magic School Bus Lost in the Solar System by Joanna Cole (Scholastic, 1990). In this title, Ms. Frizzle and her students get a close-up look at the moon, the planets, and outer space when they get lost returning from the planetarium.

Our Solar System by Seymour Simon (Morrow, 1992). This book offers a wonderful introduction to our corner of the universe, from the sun to Pluto.

More books you might enjoy:

Dogs in Space by Nancy Coffelt (Harcourt 1993). Frolic with these space traveling dogs and learn basic facts about the planets.

Why the Sun and the Moon Live in the Sky by Elphinstone Dayrell (Houghton, 1968). In this African folktale, the sun and his wife, the moon, are forced into the sky when their Earth home is flooded.

Earthlets, As Explained by Professor Xargle by Jeanne Willis (Dutton, 1989). The wisest of all alien professors explains Earthlets to his alien students.

One Hundred and One Outer Space Jokes by Sonia Black (Scholastic, 1990). "Out of this world" jokes for readers of all ages.

 Suggestions

Read aloud with your child the title on the next page. Invite your child to share what he or she has learned about the moon. Then ask your child to read the story to you. If your child comes across a word that is unfamiliar, help him or her use letter sounds, word parts, and context to read the word.

✱ Invite your child to make up additional stories about the moon and the stars.

The Moon

"Looks like we have a crescent moon tonight," said Bear.
"Yes, those mice are at it again," said Cat.

"What mice?" asked Bear.
"Why, the mice that eat the moon each month," said Cat. "Everyone knows the moon is made of cheese."

"The moon isn't made of cheese," said Bear.
"Yes, it is," said Cat.

"Well, if the mice eat the moon, how come it comes back?" asked Bear.
"The man in the moon makes a new one," said Cat. "That's his job."

5

"But there isn't a man in the moon," said Bear. "And even if there were, where would he get the milk to make the cheese?"
"Don't you know anything?" asked Cat. "The milk comes from the Big Dipper!"

6

What story do you think Cat would tell to explain the sun or the Little Dipper? Draw and write about your ideas.

_____ .

Believe It or Not

Way Down South

Way down South where bananas grow,

A grasshopper stepped on an elephant's toe.

The elephant said, with tears in his eyes,

"Pick on somebody your own size."

Anonymous

A Note About Believe It or Not

Curiosity is often the motivation for learning more about the world around us. And it is for this reason that the different, the extraordinary, and the remarkable capture our fancy. In *Believe It or Not*, your child will explore amazing things while practicing these reading skills:

VOWEL PAIRS: Vowel pairs that can stand for multiple sounds often pose problems for young readers. In this chapter, children will review and practice reading words with such vowels pairs.

WORDS WITH *aw* AND *al*: In the last chapter, your child read words with *r*- and *l*-controlled vowels. Here, your child will practice words with vowel sounds affected by *w* as in *draw* and *l* as in *talk*.

BASE WORDS AND ENDINGS: To decode unfamiliar words, second graders learn to look for base words with endings that have been attached. Here, your child will practice reading words with the endings *-s, -es, -ed,* and *-ing*.

SUFFIXES: In addition to endings, second graders look for suffixes that have been attached to base words. In this chapter, your child will practice reading words with the suffixes *-ful, -ness,* and *-ous*.

FACT/OPINION: By second grade, children begin to evaluate what they read. With nonfiction, readers learn about two kinds of statements—statements of fact and statements of opinion. Your child can practice distinguishing between fact and opinion in this chapter.

FANTASY/REALISM: Often incredible information can be, in reality, true. At other times information that seems logical and is presented as reality can be fanciful. As your child completes the activities in this chapter, talk about what is real and what is make-believe.

The preceding chapters presented strategies that help readers to better understand and enjoy what they read. One strategy that helps to check understanding is *summarizing.* Here, young readers use what they know about story structure and the topic and main ideas to tell, in their own words, what a selection is all about. To practice summarizing, ask questions that will help your child identify the setting, characters, plot, and/or topic and main ideas of a selection.

Tremendous, Terrific, Top Kid

Imagine a really terrific kid. This kid is loads of fun. This kid does amazing things and has a great imagination. Who is this kid, anyway? Believe it or not, it's you!

 ## Personal Best

There are a lot of things you can do that may not seem particularly amazing. But you can turn these things into incredible feats by being a record-breaker.

First, make a list of things you can do. Write down how many times you can do each thing or the amount of time it takes you to do it. Then try to top your personal best. Pick one or two things to practice. Each time you break a record, write down the new number. Post your new records for the day.

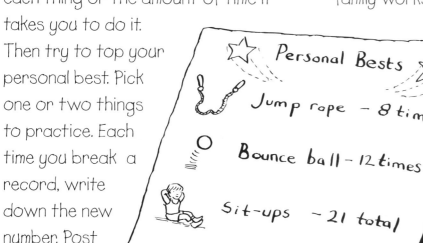

★ Personal Bests ★

Jump rope - 8 times

Bounce ball - 12 times

Sit-ups - 21 total

Get dressed - 68 seconds

Make bed - 23 seconds

 ## Family Best

Get your whole family involved! Each family member can choose one thing he or she already does well and wants to do better.

Try going for a team record! Assign each family member a task to do to complete a chore and time yourselves as you do it. Try to improve your record the next time the family works together. Here are a few ideas:

- Work together to set the table for dinner or to clear it afterward.

- Team clean a room. As an extra challenge, keep track of how many days the room stays neat!

- Time how quickly everyone gets ready for school or work in the morning. The person who gets dressed first gets the *most valuable team player award!*

Talk about personal bests with your child and help him or her set realistic goals for a chosen task.

Olympic Stars

How would you like to leap into the air to slam dunk a basketball? Or do a double flip off a diving board? Athletes do amazing things, especially those in the Olympics or on professional sports teams. Here's a chance to see yourself as a star.

"Amazing Me" Picture

If you could be an Olympic star or a professional athlete, what sport would you pick? Why? Draw a picture of yourself playing this sport. Write a caption for your picture to tell what an amazing athlete you are!

Me–The Amazing Soccer Player! I can really kick the ball far!

Write About It

Imagine that a newspaper reporter wants to write about you and your amazing picture. What kind of article would the reporter write? Write a sample article and include these ideas:

• Write opinions that tell how different people feel about the event.

• Think about the different ways these people might feel: the reporter, you, the crowd, and the other athletes.

Your child can write about a real sporting event he or she has participated in or seen. Read the article together to find examples of statements of fact and opinion.

The following pencil page practices the vowel pairs *ou* as in *loud* and *ow* as in *low* and *owl*.

Vowel Pairs: ow, ou

Who's hiding? To find out, color brown the words that have the same vowel sound as in **loud**. Color yellow the words that have the same vowel sound as in **low**.

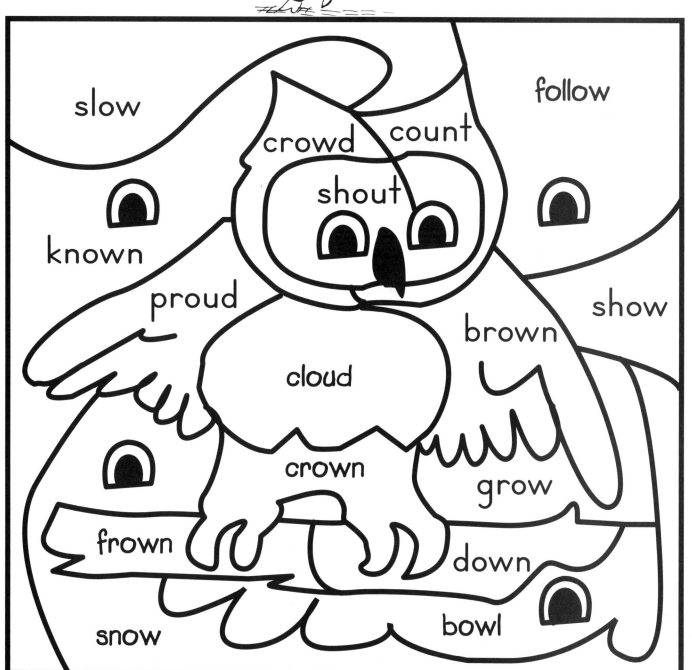

People, Places, & Things

Jesse Owens was an Olympic athlete who set six world records in one day—the most ever. The city with the most people in the world is Tokyo, Japan, with more than 25 million. The biggest piñata ever made was 27 feet high and weighed 10,000 pounds. Now that's amazing! Can you name any other incredible facts?

"Amazing Facts" Book

With a grownup, list some amazing facts. Check an almanac or a newspaper for ideas. You can also look in fact books, such as the Guinness Book of World Records.

Create an amazing-facts scrapbook!

- Staple several blank pieces of paper together to make a booklet.

- Write a fact on each page and illustrate it. Then write an opinion. (That's a sentence that tells how you feel about it.)

- As you find more facts, add them to your book.

The amazing facts in the opening paragraph come from the 1996 edition of the *Guinness Book of World Records.* Check it out!

Your child may enjoy reading the "Kids Did It" feature of *National Geographic World.* It features pictures and profiles of children and their achievements, inventions, and businesses.

An Incredible Tale

Can an amazing fact give you a story idea? It can if you ask the right questions. Let's say your grandfather can hold his breath for one minute. Do these questions give you any story ideas?

- How did Grandpa learn he could hold his breath for one minute?

- What happens to his face when he holds his breath for that long?

- How could being able to do this come in handy?

- Could Grandpa use this fact to be a hero?

Words with aw and al

Can you find the words that have **aw** or **al** hiding in these letters? Circle the word and print it in the boxes. The facts below the letters can help you.

1) O L J A W M O U T H
    A snake has a hinged jaw that opens wider than its head.

J	A	W

2) W A C H A C H A L K
    The word **chalk** comes from the Latin word **calx** which means "stone."

3) A W A L K A T L W A
    The first person to walk on the moon was Neil Armstrong on July 21, 1969.

4) M A L L O W S H A P
    The Mall of the Americas in Minnesota has an amusement park inside it.

5) W A Y T A L L H I D
    The Sears Tower in Chicago, Illinois, is 110 stories tall.

6) S W A M A C R A W L
    You can crawl on your hands and knees or swim the crawl.

My Hero!

What's a hero? A person who saves a life? A person who shows great courage? Someone who is tops in a sport or profession? A hero can be different things for different people. Let's learn more about **your** heroes.

Name Your Heroes

Make a list of people you know and admire, people you'd like to be like. What makes these people special? Are they kind? Brave? Helpful? A hero might be a grownup who is always there to help you. Or, it might be a teacher or coach who has taught you a lot.

Create certificates to honor your heroes. Write a message on a sheet of paper. Then decorate the certificate.

In the News

Ask a grownup to help you check the newspaper for heroes or heroic acts. What kind of people do you find? Did you read about police officers and firefighters? How about sports stars and actors? Are there other people you'd include as heroes? Why?

Write About It

Write this sentence starter on a sheet of paper:

A hero is _____.

With a grownup, brainstorm a list of endings for the sentence. Talk about the different things a hero can mean to you.

Invite your child to write a letter to his or her hero, explaining what it is that makes this person special. Help your child address and mail the letter.

How your child defines a hero is a matter of opinion. Most children see heroes as brave and courageous or "superhuman." Discuss how heroes can also be dedicated to a cause or belief. A neighbor who cleans up a vacant lot is a hero to a neighborhood. A teacher who helps a student is a hero. A parent who makes time to be with his or her child is a hero!

Base Words & Endings

Read each sentence and write the word that completes it. Then answer the questions.

1) In the spring, Ana and Mark __planted__ pumpkin seeds.

   plants   planting   planted

2) Soon little plants were _____ up from the ground.

   sprouts   sprouting   sprouted

3) All summer, Ana and Mark _____ the plants.

   waters   watering   watered

4) Pumpkin vines were _____ all over the garden.

   stretches   stretch   stretched

5) The biggest pumpkin was _____ to the longest vine.

   attaches   attaching   attached

6) Dad _____ Ana and Mark to enter it in a contest.

   want   wanting   wanted

7) Do you think Ana and Mark's pumpkin will win?

   _____

8) Is there a gardening hero in your family?

   _____

Incredible Fun!

You don't have to be a scientist to grow crystals or a magician to write an invisible letter. Just follow these directions and be prepared to have a little fun.

Crystal Gems

What do you need to make crystal gems? You'll need:

- 1 cup water
- 1 cup sugar
- a few coffee stirrers

Once you're ready, follow these steps:

- Pour the water into a small saucepan.
- Ask a grownup to place the water on low heat and stir it as you slowly add the sugar. The grownup should heat the mixture until all the sugar dissolves.
- When the sugar is dissolved, have your grownup helper pour the sugar water into a jar.
- Put a few coffee stirrers in the jar. Then set the jar in a warm place for several days.

Look at the jar each day. How many days does it take for the water to evaporate? What do you think the crystals on the coffee stirrers are made of?

Invisible Messages

To send an invisible message to a family member or friend, try these ideas!

- Use an unlit, white candle as a pencil and write a message on white paper. Tell your friend to rub a pencil gently back and forth over the message to see the invisible words.

- Use lemon juice to write a message. To read the message, your friend will need to hold the note by a warm light bulb. Watch as the lemon juice turns yellow and the words appear.

You may recognize the crystal gems in the first activity as rock candy, an old-fashioned treat. For the second activity, a wax pencil or a white crayon works just as well.

After your child finishes the following pencil page on suffixes, encourage him or her to use the words in oral sentences.

Suffixes

Match the words in the box to the meanings listed below. Then write the words by the matching numbers to complete the puzzle.

beautiful   lightness

happiness   dangerous

hopeful   famous

stillness   joyous

ACROSS

3) full of beauty

5) having danger

6) being still

7) full of hope

8) having fame

DOWN

1) being happy

2) having joy

4) being light

Inventions

Did you know that Louis Braille, who was blind, began working on a special alphabet for the blind when he was only 12 years old? Today, his alphabet of raised dots is called the Braille system. Kids have done some pretty amazing things. And you can, too!

◑ My Invention

Most inventions come about because people see a need for something or want to improve something that already exits. Look at these inventions:

- John Friedman noticed that when his daughter sat at a table, she was too short to drink through a straw. So he invented a bendable, plastic straw.

- Mary Titcomb worried that families living far from a library wouldn't be able to check out books. So she designed a rolling library that was America's first bookmobile.

Come up with your own invention! Remember your idea can be new, or it can improve on an old idea. Here are some questions to help start you off:

- Is there a kitchen tool you wish were easier or safer to use? How could you change it?

- Does the shoulder strap of a car's seat belt bother you? How can you make it more comfortable?

- Is there a task someone in your family complains about? What could make this task easier?

Once you have an idea, draw a picture of it. Maybe ask a grownup to help you build a model of your invention. Talk about ways to make the invention even better.

The inventors mentioned on this page are included in the science section of *The Macmillan Book of Fascinating Facts*. For more information, see "Books to Share" on page 80.

"Necessity is the mother of invention." You are the person best able to help your child zero in on needs that might inspire an invention. For example, is a longer arm needed to reach a light switch? A stuffed glove attached to a ruler might be the helping hand your child needs.

Kitchen Wizard

Over 200 years ago, the Earl of Sandwich was busy playing a game with some friends. He was hungry but didn't want to stop playing to eat, so he asked for some roast beef between two slices of bread. Can you guess what food the Earl invented? That's right, the sandwich!

🕐 Super-Duper Sandwich

A kitchen is a great place to invent new food. Start with your own sandwich.

How do you invent a sandwich? Begin by looking in cupboards and in the refrigerator for foods you can put between slices of bread. Be creative!

Pick a few ingredients to put together in a sandwich. Try these combinations:

- cream cheese and raisins (or olives),
- peanut butter and banana (or honey),
- tomato and cheese (or cucumbers),
- tuna fish and pickles (or potato chips).

Which "Super-Duper Sandwich" came out best? Create a name for that sandwich. Then write down your recipe and share it with friends.

🕐 In the Bag

A super-duper sandwich deserves a super-duper lunch bag. Start with a plain paper bag. Then decorate it with markers, stickers, or other trimmings you might have. Use your super-duper lunch bag to take your super-duper sandwich to school!

Your child might also enjoy inventing his or her own omelet or pancake combination. Add directly into the egg or pancake batter.

Books to Share

Here are some books with amazing facts and stories to explore.

What Do You Do When Something Wants to Eat You? by Steve Jenkins (Houghton, 1997). Take a walk on the wild side to find out the fascinating and unique defense mechanisms animals use to escape from danger.

Everyday Mysteries by Jerome Wexler (Dutton, 1995). Full-color photographs of everyday objects explore distance, perspective, and light and present readers with mysteries that are fun to solve.

On the Day You Were Born by Debra Frasier (Curtis, 1991). In simple words and colorful collages, natural miracles of Earth extend a welcome to each member of our human family.

This Is the Way We Eat Our Lunch by Edith Baer (Scholastic, 1995). This companion book to *This Is the Way We Go to School* takes readers on a tasty world tour to discover what children eat for lunch.

More books you might enjoy:

Guinness Book of World Records (Guinness Publishing). Published annually, this book of records has been a favorite of kids and adults for years.

Our Amazing Animal Friends by Gene S. Stuart (National Geographic, 1994). Fascinating facts about record holders in the animal world, including the largest lizard and the fastest mammal.

The Macmillan Book of Fascinating Facts: An Almanac for Kids by Ann Elwood and Carol Orsag Madigan (Macmillan, 1989). A collection of articles, lists, and facts on a variety of subjects.

The Top Ten of Everything by Russell Ash (Dorling Kindersley, 1994). The top ten of everything from natural wonders to human accomplishments.

*MY Story Suggestions

Read aloud with your child the title on the next page. Then read the first story frame. Discuss whether it's possible for Dog to stand on one paw. Then read the story together to check your child's predictions.

✱ If your child has trouble completing the final frame, ask him or her to summarize the story to tell how Dog was able to stand on one paw. You might also demonstrate by putting a finger on the floor, gently placing one of your feet over it, and saying, "See, I'm standing on one finger."

My Story

Believe It or Not

"Believe it or not," said Dog, "I can stand on one paw."
"What?" cried Cat. "You cannot."
"I can," Dog said. "And you can, too."

"Like this?" asked Cat.
"No," said Dog. "You can't hang from something."

"Like this?" asked Cat.
"No," Dog said. "You can't lie over something."

"I can't do it," said Cat. "It's impossible."
"Look, I'll show you," said Dog.

"First, put out one paw," said Dog. "Then take another paw and stand on the first paw. See? I'm standing on one paw."

"You did it!" said Cat with a laugh. "And I can do it, too."

Believe it or not, you can stand on one finger. Can you figure out how? Draw and write about your ideas.

_____ .

Tell Me a Tale

CHAPTER 6

Follow the Drinking Gourd

When the sun comes back,

And the first quail calls,

Follow the drinking gourd.

For the Old Man's waiting

For to carry you to freedom.

Follow the drinking gourd.

Traditional, African American

Tell Me a Tale

As children broaden their cultural literacy, they move beyond nursery rhymes and fairy tales to embrace our country's tales, legends, and lore. The activities in *Tell Me a Tale* invite children to explore the rich heritage of the United States while practicing these reading skills:

VOWEL PAIRS: In this chapter, children will practice reading words with the vowel pairs *oi* as in *point* and *oy* as in *boy*.

BASE WORDS AND ENDINGS: In the last chapter, children practiced reading words with endings, such as *-s, -ed, -ing, -er,* and *-est*. In this chapter, the emphasis is on **writing** words with those endings.

SEQUENCE: By second grade, children are able to identify the beginning, middle, and end of a story. Oftentimes, however, they need practice in retelling or writing stories to reflect this order. Here your child will practice creating sequences by writing and telling his or her own tales.

CAUSE/EFFECT: Second graders know that one action often causes another. As your child explores folktales and legends, he or she will sharpen this skill.

Throughout this book, your child has used reading strategies to better understand and enjoy what he or she reads. One final reading strategy children use is *self-questioning*. Here, readers are invited to set their own purposes for reading by asking questions they hope a story or selection will answer. The following are sample questions your child might ask when using all the different reading strategies:

- **make predictions:** What will the story be about? What will happen next? How do I think the story will end?
- **think about words:** Can letter sounds or picture clues help me read this word? Can the context, or sense, of the sentence help?
- **monitor:** Do I understand what I am reading? What can I do to help me understand?
- **evaluate:** How do I feel about what I've read? Would I recommend this to a friend?
- **summarize:** Who are the characters of the story? Where does the story take place? What happens in the beginning, the middle, and at the end?

Tell Me Why

Why does the opossum have a bare tail? How did thunder and lightning come to be? Let's see how Native Americans answered these questions.

Why and How

The Native Americans told many stories about how things came to be.

- The Cherokee say that Possum lost the beautiful fur on his tail because he bragged about his tail so much. One day, Rabbit tricked Possum into using a special mixture on his tail to make the fur silkier. Instead, all the fur fell out!

- Another story about Possum tells how he burned all the fur off his tail when he tried to capture the light of the sun. How do **you** think Possum lost the fur on his tail? Make up a story about it. Or, ask your own **How?** or **Why?** questions about an animal to tell a story.

Tell the Story

Share your story with someone else. Before you do, practice telling it. Here are some storytelling hints:

- Try using a different voice for each character.

- Include hand actions and facial expressions to show how the characters feel.

- Make sure you tell the events in the right order.

- Speak in a loud, clear voice.

A retelling of the Cherokee "Possum" story is featured as the *My Story* selection at the end of the chapter. Your child may also enjoy reading "Why Possum Has a Naked Tail" from *Native American Animal Stories* by Joseph Bruchac and *How Thunder and Lightning Came to Be* by Beatrice Orcutt Harrell. Other titles include *How Rabbit Lost His Tail* by Ann Tompert and *How Turtle's Back Was Cracked* by Gayle Ross.

Your child may also enjoy listening to Rudyard Kipling's *Just So Stories* for more ideas on how animals came to be. These short and entertaining tales answer the question *Why?*

You Can't Trick Me

Many of the stories people enjoy and tell are trickster tales. You can probably guess that someone gets tricked in such a story, but who? Let's look at one old folktale to find out.

◐ A Trickster Tale

There's a folktale told in the bayous, or swamps, of New Orleans about how alligators and dogs don't get along. A short version of this folktale appears on the next pencil page. Take a few minutes to work on the page and read the trickster tale. Then come back to this activity.

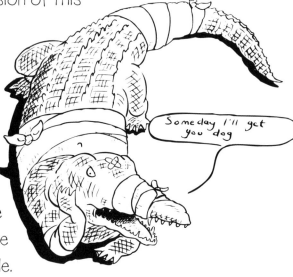

Someday I'll get you dog

Did you read the trickster tale? Now you know how Dog tricked Alligator. Can you think of another story that tells how Dog might trick Alligator? How about a story where Alligator finally tricks Dog?

There are trickster tales about foxes and rabbits, coyotes and rabbits, opossums and snakes, and many other animals. There are even trickster tales about people!

◑ A Trickster Cartoon

Brainstorm ideas for your own trickster tale. Here's how to turn your story into a cartoon:

- Divide a piece of paper into four sections.

- Draw a different picture for each part. Make sure you draw the pictures in order from beginning to end.

- Use speech balloons, or write a sentence to explain what is happening in each section.

Help your child find New Orleans on a map. Then share the rich language of J.J. Reneaux's retelling *Why Alligator Hates Dog: A Cajun Folktale*.

If your child needs assistance completing the next pencil page, review these spelling rules with him or her:

- Drop the final *e* before adding *-ed* or *ing*.
- If a one-syllable word ends with a single vowel and a consonant, double the final consonant before adding *-ed* or *-ing*.
- If a word ends with *y* preceded by a consonant, change the *y* to *i* before adding *-ed*.

Adding -ed and -ing

Add the verb endings and write the words on the lines. Then read the story.

Why Alligator Hates Dog

It all ___started___ when Dog would bark and tease
(start + ed)

Alligator just as he was _____ asleep each night.
(fall + ing)

Alligator would gnash his teeth, but Dog would stay just out of reach.

Alligator _____ he'd get even with Dog. The
(promise + ed)

day came when Dog _____ Rabbit into Alligator's
(chase + ed)

watery hole. Dog was _____ and Alligator was
(trap + ed)

_____ to eat him.
(go + ing)

Now Dog was clever. He said he _____ to invite
(want + ed)

Alligator to dinner. Alligator wasn't as smart. He was so

_____ that he let Dog go.
(please + ed)

That night, when Alligator _____ to Man's house,
(crawl + ed)

Dog was _____. Dog _____ until Man
(wait + ing)   (bark + ed)

came out. When Man began _____ Alligator's snout and
(hit + ing)

Dog began _____ Alligator's tail, Alligator quickly
(bite + ing)

_____ back to his hole in the bayou.
(hurry + ed)

And ever since, Alligator has _____ Dog.
(dislike + ed)

Tall Tales

Can you name the greatest lumberjack of all time? How about the greatest cowboy or sailor? Find out by reading some tall tales!

🕐 Tall-Tale Heroes

What's a tall tale? It's a story about a character who does big and amazing things, like this:

- Lumberjack Paul Bunyan could cut down ten trees with one swing of his ax. Paul and his pet ox, Babe, were so big that rain filled their footsteps to form Minnesota's 10,000 lakes.

- Cowboy Pecos Bill could ride anything and rode a cyclone to prove it. The rain that fell during the ride created the Great Lakes. (Do you know where the Great Lakes are?)

- Sailor Stormalong was an 18-foot tall cabin boy when he wrestled a monster octopus that was wrapped around the ship's anchor. Stormalong grew to be over 30 feet tall.

Tall tales usually have many words with **-er** and **-est** endings. You can practice these endings on the next page when you read about another tall tale hero, Sally Ann Thunder Ann Whirlwind Crockett.

Firefighter Sparky Burns taller than second story building faster than fire truck can blow out a house fire.

🌒 A Tall, Tall Tale

Create your own tall-tale hero. Begin by listing words and phrases that describe your character. Or, you can make a giant paper doll and write your list on it.

Work with a partner to help you create a tall tale about your character. Begin the story. Then ask your partner to add a little more. Keep adding to the story until you have an amazing tall tale!

For a really "tall" tall-tale paper doll, roll out some brown packaging paper and ask your child to lie down on it. Trace the outline of your child's body to make a life-size paper doll.

The pencil page that follows tells about Davy Crockett's folktale wife. Crockett was a pioneer, hunter, scout, and congressman. He was also the subject of many tall-tale stories, stories that grew taller with each retelling. You can read more about his folktale wife in *Sally Ann Thunder Ann Whirlwind Crockett* by Steven Kellogg.

Adding -er and -est

Join the word and the ending in each sentence, Write the new word on the line. Then read the whole sentence using the word you wrote.

1) Davy Crockett was the (happy + est) man on the day he met Sally Ann.

happiest

2) Sally Ann Thunder Ann Whirlwind was the (hardy + est) woman he'd ever known.

_____

3) First of all, she was (tall + er) than most men.

_____

4) And her arms and legs were (big + er) than tree trunks.

_____

5) Sally Ann was (strong + er) than a team of oxen.

_____

6) Yet, she could run (fast + er) than a fox chased by hounds.

_____

7) Sally Ann could be (brave + er) than a watchdog.

_____

8) And she could be (fierce + er) than a mama bear protecting her cubs.

_____

9) Davy Crockett thought she was the (sweet + est) thing he'd ever seen.

_____

Tales of Real People

Did you know that the poem at the beginning of this chapter is the first verse of a song that contains a secret message? It's true. During the mid-1800s, an old sailor named Peg Leg Joe taught the song to slaves. The words of the song gave directions that the slaves could follow to freedom.

Tales of Real People

People like to tell stories about heroes. In fact, many of the stories, poems, and songs you know are about real people, such as:

- Pocahontas. She was a real Native American princess who helped the English settlers. One story tells how she saved Captain John Smith's life.

- Paul Revere. He was a Revolutionary War hero who rode across the countryside to warn people that the British were coming.

- John Chapman. He was known as "Johnny Appleseed," a wanderer who planted apple seeds in the midwest.

Can you think of other real people whom you have read about? How about George Washington or Frederick Douglass? What stories do you know about these people?

Write a Poem

Poems have also been written about Pocahontas, Paul Revere, and Johnny Appleseed. Try writing your own poem. Choose one of these people or another person from history. Will your poem rhyme?

The drinking gourd referred to in "Follow the Drinking Gourd" is the Big Dipper. This verse instructed travelers to begin their journey in the spring and to follow the North Star to freedom.

Sybil Ludington rode sixteen miles through the countryside from Putnam County, New York, to Danbury, Connecticut (twice the distance Revere rode), to gather the men of her father's regiment. You can read about her ride in *Sybil Rides for Independence* by Drollene Brown.

Vowel Pairs: oi and oy

Read the words in the box. Use the words to complete these sentences about Johnny Appleseed.

joy   point
choice
        soil
boy
        voice
loyal

1) As a young _____boy_____, Johnny Appleseed was known as John Chapman.

2) John Chapman was living with his parents in Pennsylvania when he planted his first apple seeds in the _____.

3) The apple trees that grew brought so much _____ to people, he decided to plant some more.

4) Then he made an important _____. He chose to travel the countryside and plant apple trees for the rest of his life.

5) Johnny Appleseed led a very simple life and always spoke in a soft _____.

6) He loved animals and even rescued a wolf who became one of his _____ friends.

7) Today, people still _____ to apple trees and ask, "I wonder if Johnny Appleseed planted that tree?"

Apple Delights

Johnny Appleseed began planting his apple trees over two hundred years ago. Remember him by trying one of these delicious apple recipes!

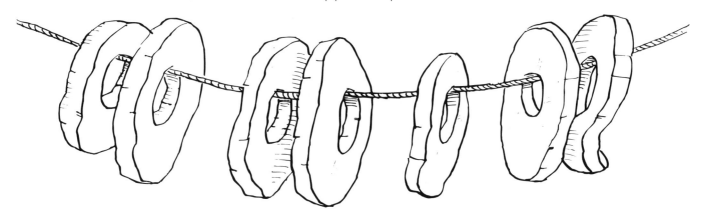

Dried Apple Rings

Grab a couple of tart, juicy apples. Ask a grownup to peel, core, and slice the apples into 1/4 inch rings. Now it's time for you to go to work.

- String the apple rings onto some twine and hang them between two hooks in a warm dry place, like your kitchen.

- Be patient. It will take a week to two weeks for your apple rings to dry. Then you'll have a tasty treat. (You'll know the rings have dried enough when they have a leathery feel and taste chewy.)

- Which do you like better, fresh apples or dried apples?

Peanut-Butter Apple Slices

Ask a grownup to cut an apple into slices for you while you get out the peanut-butter. Spread a little bit of peanut-butter on each apple slice. Enjoy this healthful snack! Do you have a favorite apple recipe? Write it down and share it with a friend.

Look at all the things I can do!

☐ I can read words I don't recognize by thinking about:

    ☐ short and long vowel spelling patterns.

    ☐ the vowel pairs **ew**, **ue**, **oo**, **ou**, **ow**, **oy**, and **oi**.

    ☐ vowels followed by the consonant **r** or **l**.

    ☐ the endings **-s**, **-es**, **-ed**, **-ing**, **-er**, and **-est**.

    ☐ the word beginnings **re-**, **dis-**, and **un-**.

    ☐ the word endings **-ful**, **-ness**, and **-ous**.

☐ I can sort things and group them together in different ways.

☐ I can tell what happens first, next, and last in a story.

☐ I can tell what is real and what is make-believe in a story.

☐ I can tell what is a fact and what is an opinion.

☐ I can name events that cause other events to happen.

Books to Share

The current attention on our nation's cultural diversity has renewed an interest in American folklore. As a result, there are many beautifully illustrated books and anthologies, including those listed here, to explore.

Iktomi and the Buzzard by Paul Goble (Orchard, 1994). In this fifth Iktomi story, the trickster earns his comeuppance when he makes fun of a buzzard.

Follow the Drinking Gourd by Jeanette Winter (Knopf, 1988). Following the directions embedded in a song taught to them by Peg Leg Joe, runaway slaves journey to freedom.

The Tea Squall by Ariane Dewey (Greenwillow, 1988). When a group of ladies, including Florina Fury, Katy Goodgrit, and Sally Ann Thunder Ann Whirlwind Crockett, meet for tea, each tale told is taller than the last.

Paul Revere's Ride by Henry Wadsworth Longfellow (Dutton, 1990). Ted Rand's detailed watercolors complement the famous narrative poem re-creating Paul Revere's midnight ride.

More books you might enjoy:

American Tall Tales compiled by Mary Pope Osborne (Knopf, 1991). Tall tales about such folk heroes as Paul Bunyan, Pecos Bill, Sally Ann Thunder Ann Whirlwind Crockett, and John Henry.

From Sea to Shining Sea compiled by Amy L. Cohn (Scholastic, 1993). More than 140 folk songs, tales, poems, and stories reflect America's multicultural history.

How Rabbit Tricked Otter: And Other Cherokee Trickster Stories by Gayle Ross (HarperCollins, 1994). Stories that bring together the many sides of Rabbit, the Cherokee trickster-hero.

The People Could Fly told by Virginia Hamilton (Knopf, 1985). African-American folktales of animals, fantasy, the supernatural, and the desire for freedom.

*My Story Suggestions

Read aloud with your child the title on the next page. Ask what he or she knows about opossums. You might mention that these shy animals come out only at night and often "play possum," or pretend they are dead when they meet another animal or person. Ask what your child hopes to learn about opossums by reading this story.

✳ Invite your child to create a story that tells why the opossum "plays possum." Read the last frame of the story again, if your child needs ideas.

Possum's Beautiful Tail

"My tail is beautiful," Possum bragged. "It's so beautiful, I get to speak at the meeting tonight."
"That's wonderful," Rabbit said. But he didn't mean it. Rabbit was jealous because his own beautiful, long tail had been cut short in a fight with Bear.

Possum bragged some more. "Everyone loves my tail. How would you like to brush it for me?"
"Okay," said Rabbit. But he didn't mean it. Rabbit had a plan that would stop Possum's bragging.

"Possum," Rabbit said, "I have a special lotion that makes fur shiny. Should I put some on your tail?"
"Oh, yes, please," said Possum. So, Rabbit put some on Possum's tail.

"Now, what are you doing?" asked Possum.
"I'm covering your tail so the lotion can work," Rabbit said. "But you musn't uncover it until tonight."
"Okay," Possum agreed.

"It's time to uncover my tail. I can't wait to see how beautiful it is!" said Possum. "Everyone will wish they had a tail just like mine."

"My tail! My beautiful, tail!" cried Possum.
"I don't think you'll be bragging anymore!" laughed Rabbit. "Wait until the other animals see it!"
"What will I do?"cried Possum?

What do you think Possum will do when the other animals see his tail? Draw and write about your ideas.

_____.